MY WAY

MY WAY

Dealing with Challenging Behaviour and Learning Disabilities

Wider Knowledge = Greater Understanding = More Options and a Brighter Future

Adam Garland

authorHOUSE®

AuthorHouse™
1663 Liberty Drive
Bloomington, IN 47403
www.authorhouse.com
Phone: 1-800-839-8640

First published by AuthorHouse   05/04/2011

ISBN: 978-1-4567-7828-6 (sc)

Printed in the United States of America

Any people depicted in stock imagery provided by Thinkstock are models, and such images are being used for illustrative purposes only.
Certain stock imagery © Thinkstock.

This book is printed on acid-free paper.

Let's start by attempting to overlook your own emotional influences and read through this book with an open mind in order to objectively take a positive step into tomorrow!

Chapter Headings

Briefly my angle

Continuity as a sanctuary, tool and key

Gain the trust, use the trust, maintain the trust

Reasons are reasons not excuses

Self control is the ultimate lesson

Become the Instructor

In order to maintain confidentiality all names of students and their family members have been changed throughout his book. Also after each case study, I have placed all of the information comprised within my explanation into a 'Table of Analysis' which is a similar table to the ones I use after any review and/or observation I do.

Acknowledgements

CREATING THIS BOOK has been an ambition of mine for some time but would not have been possible if it wasn't for the honesty, insight and support of the individuals, families and professionals I have worked with over the years. As well as this, special acknowledgement must also go to my family and close friends who have helped me reach this point.

Eleanor Lawrence and the girls of the Jolly Sailor—proof reading and related topical discussions

Emily Onley—proof reading and constructive suggestions

Claire and Michelle Hysom—photography and cover designs

HannaMarie Cook—title choice and final draft audience

Special Olympics St Albans—support and experience

Thank you to everyone who has helped, advised and supported me!

Briefly my angle

MY NAME IS Adam Garland. Some may consider me young but I have spent many years working with children and adults with special needs. I have worked in schools, colleges, sports groups, residential holidays, private homes and family holidays, and have worked with individuals from the ages of 5 and 6 up to some students in their early 80's. So as you can see there have been a fair few bases covered. Having a social life which revolved mostly around the night time, I have spent a lot of my time working, which means I average about 3 jobs at any one time, as well as volunteer positions.

As my experience grew I became highly interested in working with individuals with Autistic Spectrum Disorder (ASD). For me it was the observational side which intrigued me. Attempting to figure out how the mind of this intelligent individual worked; What made him tick?, Why he presented such 'odd' behaviours? And why oh why if he was so smart, why did he struggle so much with socialising and listening? Also being a male in a predominantly female industry I would often be asked to assist with some of the more volatile students, I can only assume because people thought I was stronger. With a lot of my early contact being with individuals with ASD this only worked to feed my interest as to the ultimate question of why! Having a high pain threshold and deciding to take up courses and conferences on the subject rapidly allowed me to develop my understanding of the issues faced by some of the students I was working with as well as equipping me with the means to help these individuals. Having first hand contact and the flexibility to attempt different strategies depending on the student, one thing became very clear to me . . . . the power to make or break a strategy lay with the parents, families and staff—and their ability to *understand* the situation. Those families who were open to new ideas and were willing to really put the effort in had fantastic and long lasting results. Not always nullifying the behaviour with the first attempt but at least being able to understand more of it. And as we were all taught at school, knowledge is the key. Unfortunately, I came across many families who hadn't had enough support, didn't have extended family to help and/ or just had low confidence and self esteem. This is part of the reason I wrote this book, to remind parents that whether your child has special needs or not, you are in control. It's up to you what your child can or can't do, it's up to you what they access and what they don't, but most of all it's up to you as to how they turn out, where their future lies and what options they have!

Life is as unpredictable as the pattern of a snowflake and so, children and adults with a learning disability (especially ASD) and challenging behaviour need to be subjected to a variety of situations in order to learn flexibility as rapidly as possible. They must realize that they are a part of this world . . . . not the centre of it. If you want the person you are thinking of now, to have the best shot at a 'normal' life full of choices, decisions, freedom and fun, then start as soon as you can—it's never too early or too late!

A stable routine is in all of our lives; wakeup—eat—sleep. Yet surrounding these routine tasks are inconsistencies, all of which shape our existence as highly intelligent mammals. Our ability as a species to socialise, analyse, create and destroy is what makes us human. Just because an individual may struggle with some of these aspects does not mean they cannot learn or should not be given the opportunity to learn. Our personality is what makes us individual, for some this means jest, for others it may mean arrogance, optimism, selfishness or simply embracing life. An individual with special needs, learning difficulties, disabilities, or whichever title you choose, has no more or less right to the basic human entitlement to be different. They may just need a helping hand to experience and see both sides of life's coin.

I have to make this very clear, even though I will mention it throughout, the strategies I use and methods I choose are the way **I** find best to work, clearest for my students and best for all in the long run. My strategies are not for everyone. Not everyone will agree with my theory and not everyone will agree with my technique, but I find it works. If you use another option and it gets the results which that child or adult needs for their future then no, it doesn't need changing and no you don't need to back track and start again. There are always 101 ways of completing any task. It's just that I know my way can work—that's not to say that others don't. Also as I'm not contracted by anyone I don't have to sell a specific system, which is not to say that everyone is. This is simply another option so as parents and professionals you can have all the options at your disposal and choose the best for your student/child/athlete.

Continuity as a sanctuary, tool and key

TO FEEL TRULY safe and secure an individual seeks familiarity. Women and men often find themselves choosing partners similar in personality to their parents not through conscious choice but because of the inner desire for security. An individual with ASD will, most likely, have an activity or task which he or she favours above all, as we all do. However, within the stringent repetition is found reliability, the knowledge of the next step before it is taken. Knowing what's to come next gives a person a sense of relaxation, an air of weightlessness. For an individual with ASD there is, no doubt, this same sensation. It can be so powerful that in a world filled with uncertainty a person can loose themselves in a separate world filled with predictability. How often have you been reading a book or writing a letter and found yourself 'loosing time'; an hour going by when you thought it was merely 15 minutes? This ability to block out your surroundings, noise and movement, is a skill which, for some individuals with ASD and other disabilities, is a lifeline. Unfortunately, society is not in a position, at present, to allow a person all the benefits of their surroundings without being part of it. Which is why, with this information, we are able to assist these individuals to cope with much of this world. Using continuity of actions, people or instruction you can enable an individual to begin to adapt. Any new task at the start isn't easy and the average child (no matter what their difficulty) will rebel, as with change comes much insecurity. However, with repetition a much stronger bond will be made. As you safely take an individual to 'the edge' and back, to their safe distance and beyond, and return to your starting point safe and sound, the points of unlimited trust begin to mount.

Continuity is a vital part of any and all activities, especially at the start. The focus of any activity can be lost if an individual becomes highly confused, as they retreat to the opposite of confusion in the other world, the one of predictability. This is why when attempting a new activity, it is essential to start and finish as similarly as possible each time. This is for two main reasons; firstly, so the individual knows when the task is to start and when it has finished, secondly because that phrase or action signifies that its okay—time to relax. It works exactly the same as crossing a bridge over a valley. You start on a hard surface where you feel safe and secure, you struggle and get nervous in the middle, and end back in a safe and secure place. This is also a position to make a very important point, because the more times you cross that bridge, the less you are nervous and struggle, until you reach a point where that crossing is just another walk and doesn't concern you at all. This is much the same as any new activity will feel for the child or adult. The only difference being that, the individual will more than likely need time afterwards, time to reflect and relax in their own world. Here begins negotiation!

If you speak to any professional who has a lot of experience with individuals with ASD (no doubt you are thinking of a few now) they will tell you, in no uncertain terms, how important structure is. Mostly because that is what they have been taught, shown and also told by individuals with ASD who have the ability to speak their mind. I am in no way saying this is incorrect, because that would be a lie. However, what is to stop us demonstrating another method of continuity? Maybe not the continuity of place, route, timetable and means to an end, but the continuity of people. Yes, I know what you're thinking . . . . "There is no continuity in people, we're all different. You said that earlier!". True, but let's reflect on why an individual with ASD might find the need to retreat to their own world?—Predictability, reliability and trust. So, what's to stop us creating this effect ourselves? Simple tasks such as doing exactly what you say, being upfront, honest and explaining issues, will make you, as an individual, reliable and trust worthy. As a human you can never be predictable, but how much of life is? Is it not better for all that an individual with ASD learns to place some of the confidence he or she may have in objects and routines, in us? Yes, it takes longer, yes, it's harder, but is it going to be more beneficial for that individual in the future? . . . . Oh yes!

When I speak to individuals with ASD, most of which are regarded as high functioning (to me there are no levels, you're either ASD or not), or professionals who have close 'friendships' with similar individuals, many of the same comments come out. "My childhood was awful", "My parents didn't accept me for me", "School was the worst time in my life". I can't help but think, yes, that's terrible, an appalling way to treat someone because they are different, but, I also can't stop thinking about the fact that, could it be some of these horrible experiences, some of the dreadful situations they were pushed through have aided them to reach the level they are at now? The ability to explain and express your feelings not only to close associates in 1 to 1 settings but also to huge audiences all over the country is hard. ASD or not, I have friends and family who would seriously struggle with that. Surely those horrible experiences showed those individuals the other side. I am not suggesting that we force our kids or adults into these situations, but creating a set of circumstances which allows for the gaining of experience can't be wrong. Maybe I'm completely off with that way of thinking, but it just seems very coincidental that those individuals seem to have fully experienced both lifestyle options, seen that it is necessary to be part of this world (society) but not all the time and have settled into a mutually beneficial negotiation.

As much as continuity is of vital importance, I see it more as a means to an end, a teaching tool. With all of the students I work with, I work very hard to gain their trust and demonstrate that I am someone they can rely on. I do this by starting every new obstacle or difficult situation with the same basics. Now even though I use a set selection of basics it doesn't mean that they are the only ones that work, as everyone is different. It works very much on a horses for courses footing. Personally, I tend to start by using a simple, regular, short outing. A place or route that the student has done many times before with no issues and knows well. A perfect example of this is a male teenager I did some work with because he was becoming aggressive towards his parents. They needed help as the aggression was becoming completely uncontrollable and extremely dangerous and they were at a loss for what to do, and were also making enquiries with residential units. So, through a friend of a friend, they asked me to see what I could do. They loved their son and didn't want to have to send him away. Therefore, I started with a classic leisurely chat at their home with Paul a couple of rooms away. This gave me the perfect opportunity to see exactly where they thought the problems lay and also what intimidated/scared them. After chatting with Paul's parents it became very apparent that they were becoming scared of their own son, to the point where they were missing out on quality time together and with him, and he was just missing out. So, I decided to continue the conversation through in the room where Paul was playing on the computer, as I wanted him to see me as part of 'Team Parents'. Once our chat was complete and I had gathered all the information I needed, I was able to make an initial assessment that Paul's aggression seemed to be linked to confusion or anxiety which wasn't helped by his parent's fear of him and their own anxiety. A quick assessment, I know, but when you're only listening it's a lot easier to hear!

So, in at the deep end, I had to now see if my initial impression was correct. Having had the chat with Paul's parents I knew that he used to enjoy going the local skate park to watch the skaters, however, due to the volatile issues he hadn't been in quite a while. So, I figured it would be nice, easy outing for our first and would give me a chance to properly evaluate him without his parents, sometimes negative attitude. Now, even though the park was only about 5 minutes away, I didn't feel it was right to introduce myself straight away with the outing so I sent his parents off for a cuppa and I sat in the room, on the opposite side to Paul. Over the next 5-10 minutes I edged closer and closer until I was sitting next to him. By this stage Paul had moved to the table and was doing a puzzle . . . . Perfect! I sat just outside of his personal space and watched. Once I realised that he was collecting all of the edge pieces first, I had my way in. All I had to do now was find the next edge piece before him and hand it to him—easier said than done! Eventually, I did and several pieces later I was allowed to connect a piece. My time with Paul continued like this for the next 3 meetings until I was at a point where Paul had allowed me to work with him on a task. One evening when Paul had finished the puzzle he was on and had packed it away (having asked Paul's parents first) I turned to him and said, "Paul and Adam are going to the skate park". Obviously, the 3 points I wanted to highlight were him, me and skate park, so I pointed to him as I said "Paul", pointed at me as I said "Adam" and pointed to the front door when I said "skate park"—mainly because I didn't then, and still don't, have any idea what the sign for skate park is! From this instruction I received the strangest of looks. It was a cross between excitement and a strong underlying look of "who the hell are you to tell me what we are doing?" I gave him a couple of minutes for the instruction to sink in, then I got up and put my shoes on and stood by the door, just to give a visual reminder/clue. After a further minute of him just sitting and watching me I repeated the instruction; no response, which let's be honest, is a good thing; would you really have wanted him to blindly follow a complete stranger? So after about another 40-60 seconds, I picked up his shoes and placed them at his feet. I had no intention of putting them on for him but it just made my instruction even clearer. He soon put on his shoes and came towards the door and we then promptly left the house, with me stepping out of the door first. I feel small body language steps like that are vital as it makes it clear from the off that I am the leader of this outing and you are following me—harsh it may sound but important it is. Being unaware of Paul's road safety abilities I played it safe, walking between him and the road and when crossing roads I was in charge and he had to wait until I said it was safe. En route, besides safety, I did not communicate with Paul unless he initiated it—touch, eye contact, movement towards me, anything I copied in order to begin to gain his trust and inclusion by communicating on his level. This is also known as Intensive Interaction.

Once at the park, Paul moved to a nearby bench where he rocked, flapped, jumped, even squealed a couple of times and became thoroughly excited at watching the skaters. On more than one occasion I again copied his behaviour to demonstrate, in his language, that I was also happy. After about 30 minutes, I stopped and turned to Paul and said "It's time for Paul and Adam to walk home", again using the same basic visual prompts as before. He was not happy with this decision and I received a very quick push to the shoulder as a clear declaration of "NO!" At this point I rapidly stood up in front of him, looking straight at him with my disapproving facial expression. Now my disapproving facial expression is a difficult body language display to explain. Possibly the best way of describing it is if you look in the mirror (obviously not right now because you're reading, but when you get a chance!) and say in your head, with real conviction "What the hell do you think you're doing?" and that's the face! Anyway, the reaction from this immediate, stern combination of body language and facial expression was met by a perfectly still teenager sitting there, looking up at me as though I was the tallest person he had ever seen and he was merely a child. Now, I know what you're thinking, "Oh Adam, you're mean . . . .", "You upset him", "That's cruel" And, yes, that is one way of looking at it, but then I feel you wouldn't be looking at the entire picture. I had to disagree with his attack, even though it was only a push to the shoulder. It was still a breach of my personal space in an offensive manner, which is always unacceptable! Therefore I challenged that and opposed it, something that Paul hadn't really come across before, as everyone had become scared of him. It was a shock for him. A shock, you may have noticed, that was dealt with no words, no physical contact, just body language. Now I will continually return to this point, but I'll lay it out now anyway. *In a situation of heightened emotion (whether it is frustration, tiredness, excitement or any other) words and visual prompts or reminders can be confusing, where as black and white body language is clear and easy to understand. However (now this is the hard part) with the body language must come no emotion. There is already too much involved and it can cloud your own judgement!* Most people, even professionals, don't realise that body language is our most powerful tool, it's just that we as neurotypicals ('normal people') are so used to reading it that we take it for granted, but, for someone who is not so fluent, it can carry a very clear message if used appropriately.

Anyway, back to the, what started off to be, short example story. We returned to the house, to the amazement of his parents, unscathed. Over the course of the next couple of evenings I spent more time playing and interacting in very close proximity to Paul, beginning to share more in the games, to the degree of doing large sections of the puzzle and joining it to his, reading sections of what he was looking at and even doing impressions of his favourite TV characters only for him to then copy me. I also stretched out the duration of our trips and changed the destinations to places he hadn't been so I could assess his anxiety progression. But every time we went out I made sure to tell him exactly what we were going to do in very simplistic forms so even if he didn't understand straight away, he soon would as he could begin to link words to places. We even returned to the skate park several times, each time telling him we were going there but taking him a different route. This got him used to the fact that he could trust what I said was going to happen but sometimes it might happen in a slightly different way than he expected. Which, let's be honest, is life!

Issue	Pre-issue	Post-issue	Highlight—future awareness
Interaction	Solitary activity involvement displaying no interest or wish for social interactions. Typical ASD-type behavior, classed as antisocial.	Small amount of interaction established and potential for sharing.	Social interaction to be worked on for short periods of time, at random times, focusing on simple/basic activities already part of student's free time. Patience and adaptation are crucial. Student initiated, carer enabled with patience.
Confusion/ anxiety	Created from mixed language and complicated vocabulary. Instructions inappropriately placed making focus difficult and anxiety unstable.	Instructions followed, time taken due to a new person involvement. Appropriate language having positive effect.	Progress to be made and methods practiced on appropriate language use in a range of situations. Reduce anxiety by developing methods and in turn trust.
'Fear'/trust	Next to no trust demonstrated and potential for fear-aggression displayed.	Minimal trust built, some 'fear' still displayed— mostly due to very short period of introduction time allowance. Establishing boundaries using calm, assertive body language has begun a reduction of 'fear' and growth of trust.	Building of trust on both sides will need work. Utilizing previously described strategies and randomizing tasks with simplicity and notice will allow progression to be made. Doing what you say is essential as trust cannot be built and 'fear' reduced, if a student doesn't believe the care team. With practice and the ability to learn from mistakes will allow the care team to reduce their own 'fears' as well as develop calm assertive methods.

Over—Excitement (Not a current issue but a point of awareness)	Look of potential excitement at choice of activity.	Excitement reduced drastically due to volume of new information having to be gained from a new individual issuing instruction.	At present an appropriate amount of caution was demonstrated, however future activity tasks may well induce physically displayed excitement which due to high adrenalin levels with this area of emotion could very easily turn into a volatile outburst. Behaviour to be monitored and activity step engagement may well be necessary—instead of just saying where you're going say (example) "shoes on for skate park" so the mind will be engaged in completing a task which should reduce the effect.
Control (Not a current issue but a point of awareness)	The display of the 'leader' of the activity or task.	Order of leadership sustained, potentially due to the body language instruction from a new individual.	At present the student abided by the basics of 'following' during the activity, however, in the future the student could well take steps to 'control/lead' the activity by having the instructor follow.

| Anti-social assertive behaviour | Attempting to push the instructor out of the way in order to dictate the progression of the activity. | Behavior swiftly corrected using a calm assertive strategy in order to disagree with the behavior and re-establish the order of authority. | Behavior deemed as anti-social is simply an action not regarded as acceptable by any member of the community. Even though a push to the shoulder is not a highly aggressive action, it is still very much, an action which must be disagreed with as it's a step towards physical conflict. If left un-confronted it may be perceived as acceptable behavior, potentially then leading to a more volatile act. |

Gain the trust, use the trust, maintain the trust

NOW ALREADY I'VE explained my views on several points which can be a great deal to take in. For some, it may well be even more so if you had been previously evaluating situations from a slightly different angle. A new perspective always makes you think, whether right or wrong. However, I have already begun to cover two of the three suggestions in the title above. I've stated how I feel its best to gain trust, in much the same way I gain trust with friends and family. Working in frontline security, as a doorman or bouncer, trust is a massive part of the job and a vital necessity. You need to know that the man or woman standing next to you as your colleague is someone you can trust because when a problem arises you don't want to have to stand and think as to whether you have anyone to help or not. And yet, there is one main problem with that degree of trust . . . . There is no possible way for you to know if it's there until a situation occurs, at which point it's far too late if the trust and support isn't there. But even in those sorts of situations there are ways to test it. When you tell your colleague you're going to approach a group of young guys who seemed to have had a little bit too much to drink and you're going to ask them to just calm down a bit, it's very easy to see if that colleague/fellow doorman has one eye on you to make sure you're okay, or has moved a few paces behind you as back-up or if they've stayed as far away as possible so as not to get involved at all. There you can start to see if there is any trust to be built upon or not. Similar situations can be used with the individual or individuals you have been thinking of as you have been reading. Obviously I'm **not** saying take them into a club, put them in a volatile position and then sweep in like a super hero. But I **am** saying take your student or child or relation to a situation they find difficult then ask them to trust you and take one more step than they would have independently, and then 'hand in hand' walk them back to where they feel safe. It's no different to when you were taught to ride a bike, whoever was instructing you asked you slowly but surely to lift your feet off the floor, place them on the pedals and trust them that you wouldn't fall off. This is probably just as well explained using one of my key foundation phrases, *"Just because* *someone finds a situation difficult does not mean that you avoid it, it means that you help them deal with it!"* And that's one of the main foundation phrases/concepts for my whole methodology. Our students (I will keep saying students because I have never been blood related to any of mine, but all of the same applies if you are) cannot go through life avoiding everything they find hard, no one can. If they do then it's probably best to stop any life skills work now to avoid any unnecessary stress because the end result will be a locked room with delivered meals or a cell of some description. At the end of the day the trust we are gaining is for one purpose and one purpose only and that is to be used to enable these individuals the opportunities, options, chances and future that is their god-given right to have as a part of the human race. Okay, yes, they might have difficulty along the way or take years to be able to cope with a specific simple task, but can we stop helping them to achieve this? . . . . NO! I find it difficult to understand some people with very strong accents or students with major speech impairments, but can I ignore them for the rest of my life? . . . . No, so I try again and again and again until I'm at a point that I can understand enough of what they are saying in order to be able to communicate effectively.

Trust is a wonderful thing to have but, let's be honest, there is no way you can ever know how the other person perceives it or how strong they see it to be. The only way to possibly be able to assess that is in the practical application and what it can lead to. And yes, sometimes that may well mean a nudge in the right direction because you know they are going to be safe on the other side. A family, very close to my heart and one I spent many years working with, had this very situation on multiple occasions and it paid them dividends. I started with this particular family when I placed a small advert in the parent bulletin in the school I was working in at the time. Having reduced some of my evening working hours I soon discovered I had too much time on my hands which bugged me, I don't like sitting around. So, I thought I would put the advert out to see if any of the school's families (within the school I was working at the time) need home based respite or babysitting. One of the families that asked me, called me for a meeting at their house to discuss the potential of working with them. So after chatting for a while we came to a weekly arrangement of two evenings and the possibility of occasional work on the weekend, and I left very happy. Over a very short space of time though, it became incredibly clear that this fantastically loving and devoted family didn't really need much help, just confidence building. As you can see I do like to analyse—I did tell you! Anyway, we continued to meet up and I would either take Ray out, or stay at home with him while his parents went out or go out with them to resolve certain community-based issues. Well, the classic issue/example came not too long into our working career together and it was at the swimming pool.

I had taken Ray several times on a Sunday into the 'baby pool', he was about a year over age but the lifeguards said it wasn't a problem as they knew I was a swimming coach and that he had some underlying difficulties. He started very nervously but rapidly grew to love it, to the point where I was now asking him to trust me further by starting to teach him to actually swim, not just play, so he could be safe in and around water. *"As an individual continues to demonstrate their ability to be safe, naturally more freedom and independence will come, however without the safety there can be no independence!"* He excelled at the swimming and thoroughly enjoyed it. Our next issue however was . . . . THE BIG POOL . . . . an intimidating option for any child but, even more so, for a young child with severe autism. So I started by stretching the games, e.g.: if we were playing catch I would stand in the main pool and throw to him in the small pool. This associative play continued for several weeks getting him to the point where he would come and sit on the side of the main pool but not get in. Now this whole process could have been done a lot quicker but there was no need, he was continually progressing, there was no need to take him to 'the edge' yet and the family had no immediate Olympic bids to qualify for, so time was all in my favour. However, I soon reached a point where I felt it might be best for a quick entrance and then to help him adjust. This was primarily because he was getting too big for the small pool and, the fact of the matter is, sometimes the plaster does hurt less when you just rip it off! (I must say, soaked in water always hurts even less!) As his mother had joined us on several occasions and was the individual in the family which he trusted the most, but at the same time the one with the least confidence, I felt it would be an excellent opportunity for them to use and progress their working trust/relationship. So I started the session, as always, doing some work in the small pool and then moving onto the games which bridged between the pools. This continued onto the task of sitting on the side of the main pool, at which point I asked Ray to give his mum a hug while she was standing in the main pool. He was not happy about doing this because it took his hands off the side, but within a couple of minutes he was very confidently completing this task too. Next I told his mum that *her* next task was, on the next hug, to lift him into the main pool and stand him up, as slowly as possible so he could really feel it, know and see what was happening, once he was stood just leave him to it but give massive congratulations and praise (non-physical). Ray appreciated the average cheer but also loved "Woooooo Yeah Good Job" in an American accent—damn American computer programs! So that's exactly what we did, his mum with no hesitation went in for the hug, lifted, turned, lowered and told him to stand. He was scared, no doubt about it, but he did it, and once standing and receiving his congratulations he couldn't stop giggling and moving around his depth with ease. Now here not only had I used the invested trust in the Ray's mum but she had then in turn used Ray's trust to allow him to try and enjoy something new. We both knew he was going to enjoy it, he just needed help taking that first step, which for him was quite a big one. From there on out his ability, confidence and enjoyment has continued to grow exponentially.

Issue	Pre-issue	Post-issue	Highlight—future awareness
Confusion/ anxiety	Overall reluctance to 'take the next step', lack of awareness of purpose and task.	Grossly reduced confusion/ anxiety, full interaction within environment except for unpredictable/ over-playful touch.	The routine and unchanging pool structure will aid the reduced confusion/anxiety, but will the introduction of a new swimming pool reignite those same feelings?!
Confidence	Very low confidence in task, environment and individuals around him.	Heightened confidence, primarily in task and environment but also in family members and instructor—still unnerved when asked to complete a slightly harder task.	Confidence must continue to grow through the use of repetition and the request of 'next step' tasks. Even though low confidence is a perfectly acceptable reaction it must still be tackled as there is the possibility it could lead to complete and utter avoidance of the environment and/or any similar.
Trust/ reliability	Significantly reduced trust for surrounding assistance, especially specific family members. Unknown reliability of environment.	Trust has grown considerably to a point where anyone in the water can be trusted as long as they keep a reasonable distance. Self reliability has been discovered leading to an incredible growth in swimming ability.	Trust can be lost as well as gained, yet should be continually tested in situations which are planned and will result in a 'happy ending' in order to again establish the trusting bond. Trust/ reliability (in people) will continue to grow as ability does. The need to trust others is always there and should, therefore, be reiterated through the practice and repetition of simple tasks using the family member as a focal necessity for the task, i.e.: going out of depth.

Safety	Very limited knowledge of poolside and pool rules.	A very good and extensive knowledge of the do's and don'ts, some through first-hand experience and others through repetitive instruction.	As with any situation a majority of kids, but especially those with special needs, learn best practically. However some rules of a pool building come with dire consequences and must, therefore, be continually reiterated and monitored.
Frustration (not from Ray's side)			With a task such as this it's very easy to become frustrated because you know that the child will enjoy the experience and improve if only they could take this one little step which they won't do. Frustration is exactly what can lead to a complete breakdown of the task and a full collapse of any bond made, primarily because it leads to forcing/pushing without an impartial perspective before the individual is ready.

Some of you are probably sitting there and wondering why the use of symbols or a visual timetable wouldn't have been better. The fact is, if you were stood balancing on a chair listening to your friend but holding the wall, your trust and thoughts of reliability are invested in that wall not in the words of your friend. But if you were stood balancing on that chair listening to your friend but holding your friends hand, your complete trust and entire thoughts of reliability are 100% invested in your friend, and next time your friend suggested that activity there would be a greater chance of you being willing to do it. Obviously, no, I am **not** recommending testing relationships by balancing on a chair!

It just happens to be the best example I can think of at the moment which most people could visualize.

Now as far as trust maintenance goes, I see it as purely a matter of practicing. Call me odd if it does turn out that I'm the only person who feels/thinks like this, but while an individual is under our care, for whatever reason or duration, it's our duty to continually practice all of these life skills. The main reason for this is because when these children or adults leave our care, we cannot know exactly what they are being taught or shown or exposed to so, surely, its our responsibility to be able to leave that student with a clear conscience, knowing that we did everything humanly possible to give them the opportunity of the brightest possible future. So, the question of how do I keep the trust I've built, doesn't really need asking because you are continuing to use and build it everyday with every task. This is obviously working on the basis that you aren't taking unnecessary risks and the student *is* regularly returning to a point of security. Clearly, if the risks are too high, then the steps you're taking are too big and if the steps are too big then there are more chances that an injury could occur or the student could become so scared that you have just eradicated the trust you've created and set yourself back months of work. Similar issues can arise if the student doesn't get the chance to return to a point of security, this part is essential. It's where the negotiation lies. You can't expect a student to place all their trust in you, push themselves to the limit, fire on all cylinders only to find out they have to do it all over again straight after. Everyone, and especially our students', need down time, chill out, processing time, whatever you wish to call it. It's the only way the body and mind can recover and prepare for the next challenge. If the challenges are too close together then that's when you can have extreme outbursts as a student will fight for that down time or simply fight because they are mentally drained and at a low tolerance level. But again if you give the down time to them before they even consider fighting for it you are continuing to build your working relationship/trust. The absolute classic example of that . . . . is builders. Have you ever noticed the rapid change in the attitude and work ethic of a builder working on a hot day who is tired and sweaty, and without him asking, you bring him a glass of iced water? Suddenly he's your best mate and, within 5 minutes, you know his entire family history as well as the story of the tattoo that is indecent to show. And that's the same principle with our students, if you 'read their mind' by giving them something they need (not want, but need) after they've worked for it there is a great degree of appreciation. Some may well see this as a reward. I wouldn't, purely because my interpretation of a reward only benefits one person whereas the chill out/processing time may well help the student to deal with and think about what's just happened but will also allow their minds to relax so they're ready for the next task or to help with the next job. All of this, I have found, can and will continue to reaffirm the trusting bond, not to mention broaden the horizons and understanding for the student as well as your understanding of their perspective. Assuming, of course, that you don't go too far, becoming their telepathic slave!

Reasons are reasons not excuses

WHETHER A PROFESSIONAL or a parent it's very easy to see a situation involving challenging behavior and naturally begin to excuse the behavior by recollecting the previous issues of the day or the individuals past. Now some may call me insensitive or 'hard' but I see those previous issues as potential reasons or explanations for the behavior but *never* an excuse. A bad night's sleep, an alteration of a routine or an obscure transport arrangement are all valid reasons for any students to have a 'difficult' day, but are they valid enough to make a volatile attack justifiable? . . . . Hell no!

I must say this sort of situation is one that I regularly come across as the families I work with regularly excuse and defend their child's behavior by saying, "He's had a really long day" or "He didn't sleep very well"—have you ever found yourself saying phrases like these? As far as I'm concerned that isn't good enough, purely because if you don't disagree with that sort of behavior, even once, you are in a roundabout way saying its okay. Yes, pick your battles, as long as you are aware of the message you're potentially sending when you let an issue slide. We all have 'off' days, days where we are a little bit niggled or irritable, but how often on those days, do you turn around and hit someone? A 20 year old autistic lad I used to work with was in exactly this same situation and still living at home with both parents and siblings. His dad often worked away from home and would return late at night, a common working family situation. As a gesture of welcome both himself and his mum would stay up and greet his dad on his return, which could regularly be in the small hours of the morning. You're probably already seeing where this is going and you'd probably be right! Obviously for a 20 year old, staying awake until that sort of time isn't at all uncommon, unfortunately though the following morning he would always be over-tired, irritable and would often have several incidents at college during that next day. Now besides the fact that I never really felt the college dealt with the behavior in a very good way, what concerned me more was that upon hearing the reports of a bad day and being on the receiving end of the punches his mum would always try to calm him down with a sympathetic voice saying, "its okay, I know you're tired" and then offer him something, like a drink or cake, to satisfy him and attempt to defuse the situation. Now don't get me wrong I totally understand why she did this, and being on her own at these times it's understandable. However can you see the point at which her actions could have been seen from her son's perspective as a reward? Also, dealing with that sort of situation in that manner uses and instills no discipline or boundaries, which at the end of the day throwing punches is something that needs to be confronted. So this is where my work began.

I initially started with a conversation with Tom's mum to gain her angle and opinion on what was happening, and I really wanted to get to grips with her feelings when physical confrontations arose. It was, unfortunately, during this conversation that she began to cry (something which seems to happen quite often when I talk to parents about their situation). Obviously my initial question was "What's wrong? Why does thinking about this make you cry?" Her reply was that she was scared of him, didn't know how far he would go or what would happen if the diffusion options she gave didn't work. And that is the issue, that's why a lot of people get really hurt when situations like this arise *__With no respect comes no guarantees__* So once she had had a chance to get most of her concerns off her chest we then went to work! We arranged for me to be at the home the following evening when he arrived back from college, as it turned out that Tom's father would be returning home late tonight/early tomorrow morning, so by college tomorrow he would be in a more volatile mind set with a lower tolerance level.

When I returned the next day Carol (Tom's mum) was very apprehensive and nervous. After a short conversation it appeared to be primarily because she was concerned about me getting hurt, seemingly she had resigned herself to Tom hurting her, but was not happy with him potentially hurting someone else—a classic parental perspective mostly derived from excusing the behavior. Also not meaning to be seen as a sexist but it does seem to be mostly mothers who, for some reason, see it as part of their role to be on the receiving end of extreme reactions, rather than anyone else. Anyway, using my amazing powers of persuasion, I talked her round and we chatted about random subjects in an attempt to distract her line of thought. Shortly after, the door bell rang which created an instant alteration in Carol's body language, as her face resembled that which had seen a ghost. She darted to the door, I followed, and she was greeted by the driver of Tom's transport who informed her very quickly that he was not in the brightest of moods. A clearer expression of nervousness struck her face yet again, so I interjected and reminded her that I was here and would deal with any/all of the repercussions. I positioned myself a few feet back from the doorway in the direct path through to the rest of the house—no, I was not trying to antagonize him, but I would very quickly be able to analyze the extremities of his mood by seeing if he attempted to just barge straight through me or maneuver around. Once let off the bus Tom ran to the front door without acknowledging Carol or the mini bus driver and continued straight through, dumping his bag on route. As he came through he looked up, saw me and continued to charge straight at me. I stood my ground causing him to 'bounce' backwards. Something that, with what can only be described as the evilest stare I've ever received, he made explicitly clear he didn't appreciate. He then tried again with the same outcome, third time round Tom opted to use a little logic and respect, and decided to side step around me, enabling him to access the rest of the house. At this point I just want to be clear and state that, I wasn't standing in a rugby scrum position in the middle of the gang way, I was stood in a leaning position against the door frame to the lounge covering about half of the gap—so it wasn't a confrontational stance, just an awkward one. From there he went straight through to the living room and sat rocking while watching the music channel.

While I observed Tom, Carol was sighing frequently at the terrible day he had been having, as she read his behavior log book. Then seeing that her body language was very defeatist I told her to ignore it because tonight was a fresh start. So she continued on with her evening routine and began to make Tom a small fruit snack. Once she had done this, she carried it through to the table and sat down. Tom then promptly came over and took the bowl off the table heading back towards his position in front of the TV. Carol was very quick to say "Tom we sit and eat at the table" and that's when it started. Tom was far from happy, threw the bowl to the floor and began to charge towards Carol. At this point I moved to intervene. Tom had obviously decided it was a better option to continue the attempt to fight rather than back down (fight or flight), so he swung for me. I blocked his punch and held his arm. He then repeated the action with the other arm to which I responded as before. Then using my disapproving facial expression—the one I used for Paul in the earlier situation, I instructed him in a calm but assertive voice to "Sit down!" He continued to struggle against me as I simply held his arms, no pressure or force, just held. So I reinforced my instruction by using body language by standing straighter and taking one step towards him, as there was a chair not far behind him. He then sat, at which point I swiftly let go of his arms and took a step back. I wanted to make it very clear to him and Carol that once you've done what I've asked I will move and give you back your personal space.

Tom did continue, on more than one occasion, while sitting to not only stand back up but also to grab me. As far as the standing is concerned, I do not agree with the intention of that action until *I* have decided that the student is ready and calm enough. Unfortunately, in that sort of situation you can't usually rely on the student to know or realise when they are calm, and therefore ready to rejoin the previous activity. So, when he did attempt to stand I took a step toward him, again using my body language to reiterate my instruction and if that wasn't a clear enough communication on its own, I simply repeated the verbal instruction and/or use gentle physical touch to emphasize my desired outcome. It's at times like these when I have to be very careful so as not to teacher the wrong lesson, because if I was to use an inappropriate amount of physical touch or for too long, I could unknowingly be demonstrating that force is an appropriate form of communication—the opposite to the desired lesson. As far as Tom's grabbing was concerned, my response was to let it happen and then hold his hand while using my facial expression and body language to express my disapproval whilst slowly removing his hands, placing them back on his lap and then again taking the step back to demonstrate that he was now doing what I asked for. I feel it is very important that my students realize very quickly that trying to hurt me won't change the situation or the outcome so I ignore it and teach replacement communication methods. This is where my high pain threshold comes in very handy! Throughout this Carol was stressed, not only because Tom was distressed, but also because she didn't quite know where to put herself. So I made a point of explaining what I was doing and why, as I felt this might distract her concern slightly and place her mind more into the role of an instructor, less of a frantic mother. She also moved to clear up the mess and asked if she should get him something else because he obviously didn't want the fruit. As far as I'm concerned ***"Unless it's a sociably acceptable communication, it doesn't count!"*** Also, when Tom had earned back his free-time by calming down and being allowed to get up and go, it's his job to then clear up the mess he had made. Which after a total time of only about 2-3 minutes of sitting, including a couple of 'half-arsed' attempts to get up and leave prematurely, he did and did well with a little help from myself. Once we had tidied up, I thanked him for his help and said "Okay now you can go" as he had done exactly what I had asked of him.

Issue	Pre-issue	Post-issue	Highlight—future awareness
Excused/ ignored behavior	Challenging behavior excused and ignored due to ease and 'keeping the peace'	Behaviour challenged, rules begin to be put in place and household respect begins to be re-established.	Continued assessment necessary as this level of behavior, combined with the ease of excusing, can/will develop. Key family members need vital support and development with confidence building. *Recommend: experience instructor role with another student*
Low tolerance	Very controlling/ demanding behavior. Uses aggressive intimidation as communication.	Beginning to develop a basic understanding of calming tactics and sociable communication.	Due to sheer strength and targeted aggression, calming techniques should be practiced on a regular basis over small insignificant tasks in order to make the strategy reliable and to encourage an automated response at more crucial junctures.

Communication	Basic PECS use at college but not at home. Limited verbal ability. Use of challenging/anti-social behavior in order to answer questions, request items and explain feelings.	Use of verbal answering/requesting developed to the point of "I want . . . (name of item) . . . please". PECS brought into the house upon mother's request as backup communication. Challenging behavior no longer regarded as communication for anything else other than the need to calm down, and then appropriate communication used. Upon mother's request instructions of snack whereabouts placed at front door so visitors can also answer any socially acceptable requests.	Very important subject to continue working on, vital as a part of behavior management. Care taken so that PECS is used as back up communication and/or progression to new language development, but not as the prominent communication form! Language used by family/guests kept relatively basic until confidence and ability improves.

In these sorts of situations I feel it is imperative that you ***"Never punish bad behavior, you simply don't reward!"*** I know what you're thinking, "you did punish him because he had to sit and stay there until you said otherwise". Now my view is that, this wasn't a punishment it was a controlled environment which enabled him to calm ***himself*** down whilst still having the choice to comply or not—because, at the end of the day if he had really wanted to, he could have simply picked me up and thrown me out of the way. This, I hope, demonstrates as to how strong/effective good body language and clear communication can be. And, yes, it was a bit of a battle of wills, but only to enable Tom to experience a better way for him to deal with his emotion rather than hurting those around him. Also the thought as to why I thanked him for clearing up his own mess, may have crossed your mind. Simple, the promotion of socially acceptable behaviour through the use of an appropriate social congratulatory communiqué—in other words, good behaviour deserves a well done because bad behavior gets nothing.

Self control is the ultimate lesson

AS IT TURNS out the chapters you have already read, lead quite nicely to this point as it's the culmination and definitive point to all of the work I have done, still do and will continue to do with challenging, and extreme challenging, behavior whether associated with autism or other disabilities.

A lot of professionals and establishments use different forms of physical restraint to try and calm students, and control them. My main issue with this is simply that, when in the future will there be restraint trained staff at a bus stop or at a supermarket or somewhere in the vicinity ready to rectify a situation that a student can't handle? There isn't and there won't be!! And if there is, then that particular student is obviously being escorted and therefore hasn't got full independence, which lets be honest is the ultimate aim for any parent/carer/professional or at least should be! *"If you are always 'aiming for the stars' then every step you take in that direction will be in the best interest of the student!"* Also, I can't help but notice, that physical restraint isn't teaching the student anything except that when you kick off a group of 'us' is stronger than you, which therefore makes it nothing more than a containment tool. So there is no foundation respect for other people or genuine understanding of applicable consequence. Don't get me wrong there is clearly a consequence; if you misbehave we hold you down until you're tired, exhausted or calm, whichever comes first. Well that's my view anyway, I'm sure anyone promoting restraint will be able to come up with viable rationalizations for those steps. Personally I don't agree and feel that it's not a constructive pattern of behavior to teach or to learn. For that reason I sought other options to reach the end results that the families I worked with, and myself, wanted the students to achieve for the sake of their own future. In order to explain my perspective I will attempt to describe my findings from my viewpoint.

Emotion is probably the most difficult part of human nature to control but is often a lot easier to mask. Many of our students tend to fall into one of two brackets; either they 'wear their emotions on their sleeve' or they mask their feelings/emotions. This, as you can see, is much the same as a neurotypical individual (you and I) reacts and the delayed reactions from either of these would also be very similar. Now a student who is very open about their emotions makes the job a damn sight easier as you can clearly see tension or stress brewing. This can allow you to reduce the duration of a task (not by reducing the amount of steps to complete it!) or have stress relieving activities ready to progress on to. This will also mean having to have contingency plans at hand is less necessary because, obviously, you will have more time to prepare whatever needs to be done next. This won't, however, necessarily make the job of dealing with the behavior easy, as whichever method/strategy you use will still have to be effective, although probably not as immediate. If it makes it easier to comprehend, think about one of your friends, because everyone has one, who says exactly what they think and will be very upfront about their feelings. 9 out of 10 times you know exactly what to anticipate from their reaction and even what they're likely to say, but even knowing all of that doesn't necessarily make the aftermath of their comments easy to deal with. However, if your student is very good or naturally able at masking their emotions, the signals you are looking for are that much more subtle. Fidgeting can sometimes mean frustration or annoyance, hyperactivity can sometimes mean confusion or a low tolerance and so it goes on. But after these subtle signs can often come an 'explosion' of emotion, usually displayed as a seemingly unprovoked attack or volatile situation which needs immediate attention. To be totally honest, these are very much the sorts of signs you pick up along the way, learning by trial and error. But, as you've probably already realised, the ability to stay relaxed and focused will pay dividends when you come to try and recollect the entire situation in order to identify those potential triggers and signs. I find it is always imperative to be *"Calm but assertive"*

Anyway back to the task at hand, the reason I explained all of the above is basically because in order to teach a student when they need to calm themselves, what calm is and when they've achieved it, it needs to be taught by association. There are other methods, but as we went through before, in an emotion ridden state, things need to be made as black and white as possible to make them as clear as possible. Yes, the use of social stories or a visual timetable can be useful but, I would say, you are only talking about a very limited selection of students who can, not only deal with those options, but also can understand and use them effectively, especially during those necessary time periods. But learning by association works for all and is mostly how our students learn anyway. Hey, its how most of us learnt when we were kids! A brilliant example of this is (and be honest about how many times have you been in a situation similar to this), "Careful, that water is hot" but the student touches it anyway and has felt the heat. Now they have learnt what hot means, not because you told them but because they experienced it! I am not, for one second, telling you that you must let your students get burnt, freeze, get ill or injured, just that this is how most of our students and children in general learn. So that's why I tend to simply instruct my students to sit when they're developing aggressive behavior. Not only because they are then in a controlled position but also because I want them to recognize and feel how they're feeling, when they need to calm down. Also so individuals can feel the transition to the point at which their body is calm and relaxed. It's the same when a child is toilet training; they wet themselves—they are taken to the toilet. And over a short amount of time they are able to recognise the sensation of feeling like they're going to wet themselves, so request or go to the toilet (often not with much time to spare) to avoid the uncomfortable wet trouser stage. The same works for the volatile part of challenging behavior. When a student feels themselves getting worked up—whether it be the feeling of tightening muscles, confusion, adrenaline rush, whichever is the realization point for them, they begin to associate that feeling with sitting out. And this lasts until their body reaches that point of calm (which in the past was the time when the individual was allowed to get and go) and they can continue with whatever they were doing before their enraged feelings began. It's that associative development which allows them to know when they are reaching an uncontrollable point and need to take steps to avoid the outcome. It also means that the parent/carer/staff only need to remember one simple instruction when all begins to go wrong and your mind is a blur—"Sit down!" This in turn means that a parents/carer/staff isn't wrestling with a student and risking severe injury if a restraint goes wrong or if a student's strength is underestimated.

Over time a lot of students will begin to distract themselves to avoid the feeling or postpone the outcome. This is a very good coping mechanism and could well be a life-line for them as they progress in the future, but, during the initial stages of learning, the student needs to be fully aware of all of the emotional steps involved in the calming process. This is mainly so that if avoidance isn't an option, then fight isn't the resolution! It means the student can go through life without continually avoiding anything and everything that is a bit of a challenge, but is able to actually deal with the problem at hand and process the entire situation in order to behave appropriately—just the same way any adult has to. If a student can't deal with or process a certain situation then the unresolved emotions involved can build up much the same as masking emotions can do, so you could well end up with the explosion of volatility again anyway.

A young woman I used to work with in one of the educational facilities I regularly visited had an undiagnosed learning disability, combined with challenging behavior which displayed itself through the grabbing of hair and scratching of skin. As it happens a lot of my work with this particular young woman came after her personal break through, which was brought about by the hard and continued work by a colleague and close friend of mine. It had always been the procedure that when Charlie grabbed someone's hair, any available staff would rush over, prize her hands out and restrain her. The main issue with this was only to come to light a year or so after. When my colleague, Annie, worked with her she would regularly find herself to be a target and endured great pain when her hair was grabbed as Charlie had an amazing ability to get her fingers really tangled in the hair which made them very difficult to remove. Also, when all of the staff rushed to attempt to resolve the situation she used to clench her hands and often pull or drop to the floor, which you can imagine would have been very painful. Personally, you may well have other thoughts on this, but I feel the reason behind the pulling and dropping to the floor was the influx of all these staff and with that the, quite daunting, charge of bodies towards her. As well as the feeling of being run at there are also several different instructions being given, with different tones of voice, looking for different answers. That's not even mentioning the sensory affect of all of these different pressures on her hands and arms, as well as her body when she attempted to drop to the floor. The break through that Annie brought to this forever un-improving situation came when she was alone with Charlie in a classroom, and got caught by Charlie's lightning—speed hair grabbing hands. In the position she got caught, Annie was neither able to untangle Charlie's hands herself nor request help, one of those situations most people hope they never end up in. So with limited gentle verbal instruction and time Charlie began to calm and eased her grip. Now already this confrontation had involved no dropping to the floor, pulling or clenching of the hands—so far so good. The best was yet to come; Charlie then completely let go and sat back looking very sorry for herself. At this point most people would have told Charlie off for grabbing her hair but what Annie did was probably the best reaction she could have possibly given—she congratulated Charlie for letting go independently. I feel this really helped Charlie to identify the appropriate behavior and was one of the few positive reinforcements she had had for quite a while, a lot better than being man handled anyway. Remember "Don't punish bad behavior!" This break through soon led to her displaying her emotional distress and overload by a light tap on a person's head, which correct me if I'm wrong still has some work to do but is a marked improvement, a lot better than losing a clump of hair!

Issue	Pre-issue	Post-issue	Highlight—future awareness
Communication	Limited verbal communication but clear communication via volatile behavior. Fundamental respect for men, not so much for women.	Developing verbal communication, depleted challenging behavior.	Communication is essential to continue developing in order to highlight the unnecessary use of anti-social behaviours. Verbal communication must be shown as not only the easiest but the most efficient form of communication.
*Behavior (pre-break through)	*Distress, anxiety, confusion, etc—leading to hair grabbing, pulling, dragging to the floor, pinching, scratching, etc.	*Influx of staff on mass, potentially damaging pressure on student's hands, sensory overload. Student being told off and separated from class peers.	*No improvement, high staff ratio and no investigation into cause, primary/sole concern being containment!!

Behaviour (post-break through)	*Distress, anxiety, confusion, etc—leading to hair grabbing and pulling.	Student finding own 'end point' and developing the ability to calm themselves. Behavior leading to touching opposed to grabbing.	Steps to resolve underlying issues must now be taken in order to develop student's abilities as well as staff's knowledge of triggers. Care taken that the positive response after student has let go continues but is NOT the only access to praise. Progression to completely ignoring may be applicable—acting as though it never happened so the act loses it's 'power' and therefore attention.

*taken from 2 years worth of school reports, not witnessed by A. Garland.

Just remember, all of this was made possible because Annie allowed Charlie to reach an end point/a point of calm independently, whereas every other time previously the staff who had rushed in to resolve the incident were intervening to control the situation. It wasn't until she had been through all of the emotional steps for herself that the appropriate behavior had really 'hit home'. This is exactly what my strategy promotes. First, stopping the attack which is a necessity, purely because aggressive outbursts can seriously injure, and then providing an opportunity for the student to calm themselves every step of the way. On the very rare occasion that my hair was long enough to grab and Charlie was in an equally rare extremely challenging situation and grabbed me, I used to kneel down in front of her. She would then sit behind me and begin to brush my hair with her fingers. So with one simple move into a position of vulnerability I was able to turn an aggressive act into a relaxing situation—and I must say she gave without a doubt the finest head massages I've ever had, a skill we never knew she possessed!

Become the Instructor

NOW FOR ME, this is the most difficult part to write. In theory this is when I write down and tell you everything I feel an instructor should do, think of, remember, keep as back up and take into account. As you can imagine, this isn't easy. I'm sure you're aware that when you've been doing something for long enough there's a lot you tend do on auto-pilot. Sometimes people will often mention things to you afterwards and you haven't really realized you've done it. If you work in the care industry—you will often be quite empathetic towards others without even thinking, in the security industry—you will often monitor groups of people when you're socializing or analyze a crowd as you enter a venue, in the building trade—you will regularly 'check out' build quality when you're out and about, and so the list goes on. So now you may well understand if this chapter/part of the book comes across in places as a bit disorganized.

I suppose the best place to start at, is the observational area. This is probably one of my favourite parts of the job, as I think I've mentioned before. At this moment you forget everything you've read or been told about an individual and you just watch, something that I don't think is done nearly enough. Here you will have the best opportunity to see the world through the eyes and ears of that individual. From just watching one person you can take into account what they are looking at, what they are listening to and most importantly what triggers their behaviour. It's all well and good working with an individual and realizing a few potential triggers, it's a completely different thing when you are doing nothing but watching and with an **open mind** looking at their view point to the surrounding environment and all of its influences—you would be amazed at how much more you can pick up, just by watching. *"Observation is the key to understanding"* Also the beauty of having spent time doing observations is that, once you've done a few, you start to use those same skills when working without realizing. This then allows you to get the same amount of work done with a student but also gives you a better ability to hone in on the potential behavioural influences. My clearest memory of this, which sticks out in my mind as I'm writing, was a young lad I worked with in an educational facility a few years ago. Now he was one of you're 'text book' challenging behavior cases, in as much as several different people had tried multiple different strategies with him which had shown improvement over a short space of time but had eventually reverted back to the same behaviour being present, or a worse one being created. I was first brought onto his case because he was damaging property, injuring staff, attempting to harm other children—the classics. The difference being that, previously, he had been under the guidance of the autism specialist teacher of the institution, but she had recently left. This meant the management now had the opportunity to step in and get things done as they wanted. For Aaron this meant moving back into the classroom, as for some time the autism specialist teacher had attempted to give him full control over what he did and when, as long as he used his form of acceptable sociable communication first. This meant swimming, playground, trampette, library, computer—you name it, he got it as long as he asked appropriately for it. This is a strategy commonly used in order to reduce anxiety and promote communication. Can you see where the problem may have lied here? In my eyes he had too much control, now don't get me wrong for some students this can work very well, however, you have to really know the student to get it right. The main issue I see with a strategy like this is where was his motivation to negotiate? Why should he begin to work for you if he's already got everything he wants? Also, where does the control stop? Well, for him it didn't appear to stop at all, as his arena for control seemed to spread to wherever he felt it should—problematic or what!!

Anyway, with the start of a new term, after the summer holidays, the senior management team wanted Aaron back in class and working on objectives set by them. Now, you may think this a little harsh, but I must say I agree with their perspective, for me he had been learning some valuable lessons but in the wrong way so this needed to be rectified. So new term—new way. On the first day back myself and another/maybe two (I can't remember) members of staff directed Aaron straight through to class. As you can imagine, he wasn't thrilled about it and gave us a few kicks and half-arsed attempts to lash out. Nevertheless our main aim was to get him into the classroom, at his new work station and engage his mind, which was exactly what we did. The strategy I chose to use for Aaron was for him to access a fully laid out visual timetable so he could see exactly what was happening throughout the rest of the day in an attempt to reduce his anxiety using a basic educational format. The main issue with this, at this stage, was obviously it's my job as the instructor to make sure that what's said on the timetable, happens. ***"Do what you say!"*** Again, not only would this reduce his anxiety but also build trust and reliance. So I kept the timetable quite basic, your classic ASD timetable, and made sure that every work stint was followed by a non-work related activity. Now, seeing as Aaron always seemed to have a fair amount of energy, I wanted to give him the opportunity to expel some of this but with me still being in control of the activity. Therefore, his timetable was a typical Velcro list, which meant he would remove the top activity and place it on a separate Velcro square next to his photo—meaning that was the activity he was doing now. Once the task was completed, the Velcro word next to his photo would go into a small pouch and be replaced with the next activity at the top of the list. Aaron's timetable of daily activities went pretty much like this;

Table
Walk
Table
Playground
Table
Gym
Table
Snack
Toilet
Playground
Table
Walk
Table
Gym
Table
Playground
Lunch

Playground
Table
Gym
Table
Walk
Table
Playground
Home

You may well look at this and think it's a bit boring and on one level that is very true. However it's easy to organize, it meant that every time he was sitting at his table he was completing a piece of work, it was easy to rotate staff and most of all he knew what was happening. As you can imagine, over a very short space of time I was able to slowly but surely extend the work, either by making it harder or by giving him 2 work tasks instead of 1, and slightly shorten the breaks. Now I do say **slightly** shorten because he still had energy to burn so I wasn't going to get rid of breaks, but he had to learn how to make his free-time more efficient. This was also easy because I never stated how long the break was going to be, just that he would have one after work and therefore he also knew it wouldn't be very long until his next break. So I used the 10-0 count down to let him know the break was about to end. Obviously this also gave me the ability to end a break if there was an emergency (a crucial strategy to have in place when working as an instructor!). Already, I'm hoping you can start to see where the observation came in handy—seeing some of the potential failings of the previous strategy, realizing the best time to begin a major strategy change, creating a simple timetable after his previous time of confusion, seeing there was energy that needed to be burnt appropriately, and so on.

As time went on Aaron was working incredibly hard, to the degree that in an average day he was producing and completing more work tasks than the other 4 kids combined and his behavior had been reduced to a small squeak of disapproval—a fantastic achievement. However, the problems came when, at snack time and sometimes between tasks, he was starting to attempt to hit, kick or throw things at 2 of the other children in the class. So, the classroom staff swiftly organized an evening meeting so they could discuss the potential reasons behind this. Primarily this was to avoid the previous behavioural loop Aaron had been in, where strategies last for a short amount of time—behaviour reappears—strategy changed. Now I don't want to appear arrogant but I was pretty sure that I knew why he was doing it, but when working as part of a class team it is imperative that communication is strong and everyone's ideas and perspectives are shared—because who knows, I might have been wrong! So we had the meeting and several ideas were raised, "he's asserting himself", "he doesn't like the noises they are making", "they're getting too close", "they've got what he wants", "some staff aren't being hard enough with him"—classic comments. So, what reason would you put behind this apparent new behavior? Would it make it easier to understand if I told you that one of the target children often walked around (during his free-time) picking up objects looking or feeling them and then dropping them on the floor while making some quiet annoying sounds? And, the other would regularly stand up and walk away from the work station and/or throw a screaming strop on the floor. Does that give you any fresh ideas? Well the actual reason for this new found behavior was . . . . that they weren't doing what they were told and Aaron appeared to be taking it upon himself to correct them. I can only assume, as I couldn't read his mind, that he had spent so long sticking to the rules that he couldn't understand why they weren't and felt it was partly his job to correct this. My method for reaching this conclusion was by simply watching, seeing that he wasn't fussed about the other students until they 'stepped out of line' (did something they shouldn't) and as soon as that happened he moved round in front of them and made attempts to hit or kick them. [Now here's the interesting bit] Only because I was just watching was I able to realize that every time he moved to correct them, no matter where they were in relation to him, he positioned himself in front of the student and attempted to hit/kicked them back in the direction of the area they had just left—to me the pieces of the psychological puzzle fit quite neatly. Obviously, his perspective on correction and ours differed quite considerably as well as the fact that it wasn't his job. So I pointed this out to the other staff members several times around the snack table. Every time one of the target kids got up from the table prematurely or without being told, Aaron would get up and move towards them in quite a threatening manner. This then became a perfect opportunity for me to test my theory, and hopefully earn some more trust along the way. So, as soon as Aaron stood up I instantly sat him back down saying "What's wrong?" His response to this was to attempt to stand back up and point at the misbehaving child whilst shouting "Uh uh". My response to this was, "Okay . . . . sit down!" and I was then able to stand up, walk round the table, leaving Aaron unattended, sit the other child down and order was restored. This rapidly progressed to Aaron standing up, pointing, shouting "Uh uh" and then sitting back down un-assisted, and the situation being resolved with no further conflict. Turned out, over time, that Aaron became quite a helpful little spy!

An important point, at this stage, is that I was able to leave him un-attended to rectify the situation because he had learnt to trust me enough to sort things out. Also, I had been able to trust him to follow my instruction because we had built a confident working relationship based on boundaries and social rules. By using tools like the timetable, countdown and sometimes being a playmate during free-time, meant that those necessary rules could be established and trust could begin to be built. Now, a lot of my original observation with Aaron was done as we went along, primarily because I wasn't given much time to do anything else. But if we just look at the situation from the evening meeting, imagining all of the different strategies running through staff member's minds from courses, books, other students, other staff, and how far Aaron's behaviour and its repercussions could have gone, all due to a lack in observation. Results of injured peers, broken property, segmentation, movement to a secure placement—all of which unnecessary! I must state here and now that I don't for a second doubt the professional/personal ability of anyone who jumped to the same conclusions as the staff did in that situation. At the end of the day I've had plenty of opportunities and been in environments which have allowed me to spend time observing and practice noticing those seemingly insignificant, but crucial subtleties. If nothing else, maybe you can now see, or have it reconfirmed, as to how important observations are in helping and understanding our students, and their behaviour?!

As you can see already there are several key areas besides observation that I have described, which are essential to working as an effective instructor;

- *Analysis of previous strategies used* This is something that I tend to do automatically now but it's essential as we can and will always learn from our, or others, mistakes and triumphs. However, we can't do it without having observed those strategies in practice and having been objective about their progression. It sounds simple but you wouldn't believe the amount of time, energy and resources wasted with strategies that apply mistaken methodologies based on someone else's written version of events.

- *Timing* This is a vital part of your role as any correction or reward must be swift in order for a student to identify its relevance. As any new strategy must be well placed in order to have the correct effect. For example, earlier, Aaron knew he was going back to school which is difficult enough for some students, especially when they have assumed control of their entire surroundings, so this can often be a good time to make an extreme change so all stresses occur at one stage. However, the opposite can also be true, making small changes over a long period of time. This is why it is imperative to know your student, to have the best chance of knowing what may or may not work with specific tasks at specific times.

- *Knowing your student* Through observations and 1:1 play you can often, quite quickly, get to know what makes an individual student tick, therefore allowing you to choose the best strategy for the situation, yourself, the team and most importantly the student. Also, within this it is vital to create a safety strategy for those situations that are out of your control (a room being used when you thought it was free) and emergencies—I always favor the 10-0 countdown, others use whistles or specific words. The choice is yours but you do need one! Not only does it mean you have something to fall back on if everything else fails, but it will also give (if done correctly) any instructor a real inner-confidence because you come to know that whatever happens, wherever you are, you and your student can handle it.

- *Promoting change* Even the strictest of timetables can promote change with just a little bit of fine tuning. My earlier example of a typical autistic timetable promoted change—the fact that the break activities were not in the same order, the work tasks were unspecified and also that specific timetable moved on to include a '?' symbol which was specifically for 'something different'. I used the '?' symbol to mean that Aaron had to move to the closest adult and take their hand. We, as a team, then used random tasks to display that it wasn't a task specific symbol—sometimes we would go and deliver something to the front office, other times we would go to a different classroom or even to areas he used already just to show that sometimes it could cross over with what he already knows. We also reached a point where I could make changes to the timetable throughout the day if I needed to—case in point, fire alarm meaning a quick addition and use of '?' symbol.

¬ *Promoting team work* Staff groups, family and volunteers are all teams and parts of teams and, therefore, in order to be a good instructor you need to embrace those groups of people however much you agree or disagree with their theories, reasons or resolutions. It's crucial to utilize the team; they're vital to the student and therefore should be vital to your strategy. The fact of the matter is when a particular student is working well with you it means absolutely nothing if he/she won't work well or control their own behavior for other people or in other environments. Keeping a strong team ethic allows for progression for the student and the ability to transfer/extend trust—an essential life skill! Lets be honest it really does make you feel special when a student will only work or behave for/with you, but who is that really satisfying or helping besides your own ego?

At the end of the day being an instructor is not the easiest of positions to be in, as ***"With the ability to influence and change comes a great amount of responsibility!"*** You have to constantly make sure that everything you are doing is in the best interests of the student and their future, as well as their family, the staff and society's future. ***"No job is ever complete unless it works out well for everyone"***

The hardest part of taking on a role such as this, is what happens if you get it wrong? The answer is . . . . nothing. You just start again and make corrections. No-one's perfect and even I have to re-do strategies and re-think progression targets. We are human and getting it wrong is part of the way we learn and so it has to be the same for our students. Behaviour Management is just a posh way of saying Trial and Error!

If there is one thing I wish everyone takes away from reading this book, it is that you as an individual have the ability and responsibility to help our students as best you can. The more time our students are in the community getting it right, or getting it completely wrong but trying hard, the more knowledge there will be in the wider community, which will lead to nothing less than increased chances, opportunities and options for our students to experience. And at some point people start to realize that our students aren't that different. Despite their labels, annoying noises, difficulties and funny ways they are simply

Foundation phrases (some of the basic phrases I've mentioned and use as the basis for my methodology)

Continuity as a sanctuary, tool and key

Reasons are reasons not excuses

In a situation of heightened emotion (whether it is frustration, tiredness, excitement or any other) words and visual prompts or reminders can be confusing, where as black and white body language is clear and easy to understand. However with the body language (now this is the hard part) can come no emotion, as there is already too much involved and it can cloud your own judgement!

"Just because someone finds a situation difficult does not mean that you avoid it, it means that you help them deal with it!"

"As an individual continues to demonstrate their ability to be safe, naturally more freedom and independence will come, however without the safety there can be no independence!"

"With no respect comes no guarantees"

"Unless it's a sociably acceptable communication, it doesn't count!"

"Never punish bad behavior, you simply don't reward!"

"If you are always 'aiming for the stars' then every step you take in that direction will be in the best interest of the student!"

"Calm but assertive"

"Observation is the key to understanding"

"Do what you say!"

"With the ability to influence and change comes a great amount of responsibility!"

"No job is ever complete unless it works out well for everyone"

www.ingramcontent.com/pod-product-compliance
Lightning Source LLC
Chambersburg PA
CBHW050338290526
45785CB00006B/2542